To Julse
with love
Alexandria xx

THE HAPLESS REHEARSAL

by
Alexandria Lawrence

PEAWIT PRESS • LONDON

Published by

eawit ress

www.peawitpress.co.uk

ISBN 978 0 9570145 0 3

Printed in Singapore by Tien Wah Press

For Daniel Lewis

conductor extraordinaire

This room may be humdrum, no glamour or glitz,
Just an odd group of chairs scattered every which way.
They lie higgledy-piggledy, jumbled to bits –
Why? Whatever for? What may happen today?

The stillness is burst by a scuffling scruffle
As doors open wide – what a clamour at hand!
But what, pray, is this? What's all the kerfuffle?
With a flurry of cases... Ah, here comes the band!

They stream in from all corners, *en masse*, double-quick,
Then a slick figure bounds into the fray.
His briefcase flies open, out comes a white stick,
Up goes the baton – they're off and away!

Heads down, brows furrowed, they happen to sit
In a manner not wholly upright.
They sense that the maestro's prepared for a fit,
And hope for a moment's respite.

Blankly they stare at the cluttered black stands,
Seeing not phrases, just static old notes;
Thinking instead of their shopping demands -
Those pretty red shoes... the milk, raisins and oats.

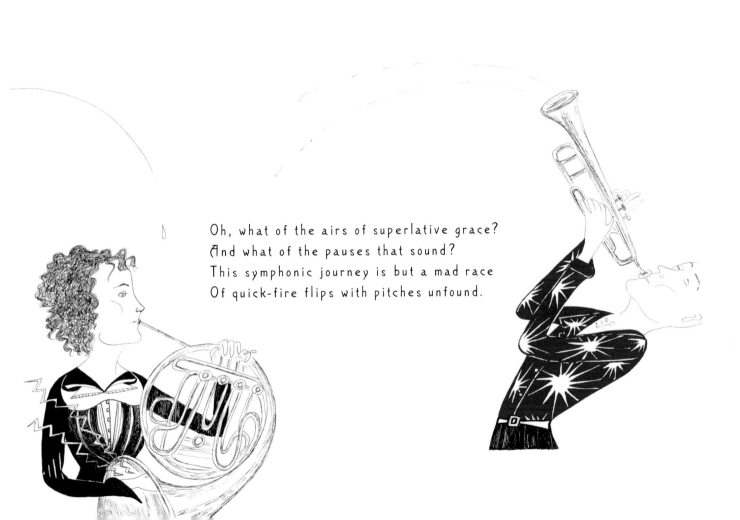

Oh, what of the airs of superlative grace?
And what of the pauses that sound?
This symphonic journey is but a mad race
Of quick-fire flips with pitches unfound.

The celli condemned for an oom-pah-pah-pah
In elegant lines of Mozartian dance
Are keenly reproached for such folly by – la,
Vi-o-lins looking uprightly askance!

The violi grip tightly their cold clammy bows,
Hesitant brows humbling their faces;
How greatly they pity their so-many woes –

Full nothing compared with the plight of the basses!

Stopped  in their tracks

from one bar to the next,

Progression is ap-pall-ing-ly slow.

The orchestra panic, utterly vexed,
As they glare at their stop-starting foe.

And what of that foe who leads this mad caper?
He at his podium steadfastly stands,
Whose devoted resolve never must taper
If that wayward bunch are to meet his demands.

His fury is mounting; the end could be near;
The quivering stick close to breaking.
Not once would he smile, ne'er smile, just sneer
With half of the orchestra faking.

At last, with one glance, a keen pair of eyes
Spy the baton not a moment too soon
And rescue the maestro from certain demise –
The effect of those heedless buffoons!

Ere those with fingers like runaway trains
Bring forth his thoughts from that sad state of bliss
To the present poor world of unprepared strains

And inform him of something far more than amiss.

"Alas," he sighs, with a subtle tut-tut,
"Why cannot my capable, well-trained hand bend
The minds of those controlled by naught but
A mass inclination to rush to the end?"

A week from the day of that hapless rehearsal
Lights in the concert hall prepare soon to glow.
But what now, oh dear, could we have a reversal?
Can the band triumph? Not a soul may yet know.

The maestro might now and then glance at his watch,
Willing the minutes to pass with great speed,
Knowing the orchestra surely will botch,
Certain that it will be dreadful indeed.

To the Auditorium

Meanwhile the audience twitter and coo –
There remain a few minutes for chitchat galore
Before silence is sovereign, discourse taboo,
And the right of free speech is with us no more.

Programme notes rustle and wine glasses clink
(a pre-concert tipple is part of the show)
As the patrons discuss the merits of mink
In adding that fine touch of class (long ago)...

Then they move on to Bernstein – a favourite of old –
And speak of von Karajan – the greatest of all –
But as for *our* maestro, they would be so bold
As to say he's up for just one curtain call.

Some say he's a chump or an old, past-it hack,
　　Whose beat is too vague, too horribly subtle.
　　　　This conductor, who once perhaps did have the knack,
　　　　　Is now just a –

　　　　"Shh!" blurts a fan in rebuttal.

Brrraahh, the brass tune as the oboe's 'A' drones,
The winds join the fray with a squeak and a toot –
Soon to follow: the strings and their stringery moans,
But now *are* they in tune? In the end that is moot.

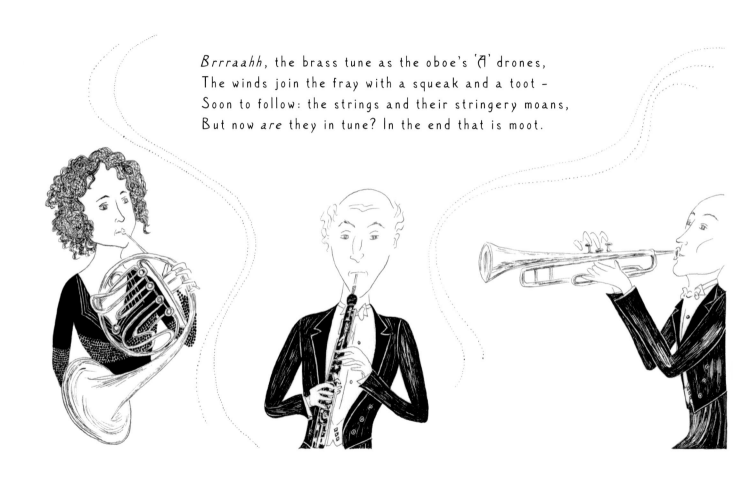

The house lights dim low and the twitters subside;
Polite applause finally fills the great hall
As the dead dapper leader appears in his stride,
In a tux, white bow tie, tails and all.

The wait now is brief – he's a no nonsense guy
Who cares not for dummy publicity spins;
The maestro appears, as a god, from on high
And, yes, here we go – hold your breath: it begins!

What follows I still cannot properly say;
Perhaps 'twas a dream, a mere fanciful flight,
Which bewilders my mind to this very day,
Which I don't understand (try though I might).

The concert begins with a most splendid passage,
Performed with rare taste, with nuance and flair,
Blooming with berries (a rather fine vintage),
Inducing all in attendance to stare.

You'd think the enchantment would ebb more than flow
As the evening moves on and the band starts to tire.
Their panache would wear off, grow progressively dull,
But their glory persists — they are fully inspired!

SAFETY

CURTAIN

INTERVAL

"Oh yes, I say, what a *mah*vellous show!"
Spouts a matronly m'am to the chap on her right
"And I'm one to judge, yes I *am* in the know –
A *vrai critique* am I and tip top 'tis tonight!"

But wait just a minute, hold the show, steady on...
Is this the same band that rehearsed just last week?
That ragged old lot with their grimacing brows
Are now these fine artists - so splendidly sleek?

Not to say it was perfect – there's the odd windy squeak,
A cracked note from the horns as they go on their way –
But, needless to say, it is Art (and not weak)
To have a few "noises" join in the affray.

That's the queue for the Ladies, which snakes round the floor,
Winding its way round each pillar in sight.

Once 'twas so long it went right out the door
And they froze in their furs on that cold, blustery night.

Blow the horn, sound the whistle – they're off once again!
Not a hiccup, a false start or technical hitch
Disrupts the fine flow that's been streaming this evening
Or lends to a feeling of dubious pitch.

The onlookers look on – they stare straight ahead,
Heads poised (quite frozen), in time and space still;
Rapt in attention – a sure sign they're well bred –
As they gaze at the stage and sit, dressed to the gills.

There's a pause between movements and, *"Erghhuh!"* they emit
Such a volley of coughs that would make the Queen blush.
It's a mystery, this urge to hem, haw and see fit
To fill every silence with... *"Shh* now, hush hush!"

Not a wasp or a fat, snorting pig at the trough;
Not a hack or a wheeze, not even a bustle...
Nothing will pierce like the innocent cough
Except for, perhaps, the malevolent *Rustle.*

The fast-changing chords near the end are now heard,
Perfectly heavenly, not to be shunned,
Which resolve on a cadence – a picardy third!
And what of the maestro? Well, he is quite stunned.

He taps several shoulders (a gentle pat pat)
And bows to the listeners, wholly with grace;
A grin, which could outdo Sir Cheshire Cat,
Spreads full across his congenial face.

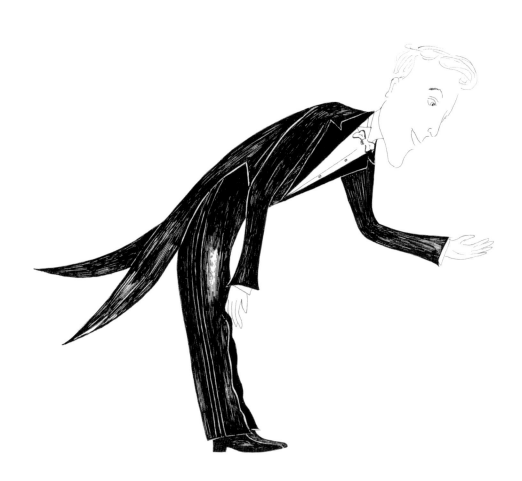

He peers straight before him at hundreds of hands,
Clapping and flapping with wild delight.
At his dark polished shoes a fine bouquet lands,
Obscured by a hazed blinding blaze of stage-light.

He turns to the orchestra, spies dripping chins
And faces transfixed: how blankly they stare!
He sees lips sealed tightly, too weary to grin,
But finds that *his* audience truly lies there.